THE A TO Z OF *Delicious* CARIBBEAN FOOD

Karlene Rickard

Published by
Filament Publishing Ltd
16, Croydon Road, Beddington
Croydon, Surrey CR0 4PA
www.filamentpublishing.com
+44(0)20 8688 2598

The A to Z of Delicious Caribbean Food
by Karlene Rickard

© 2017 Karlene Rickard

The right of Karlene Rickard to be identified as the author of this work has been asserted by her in accordance with the Designs and Copyrights Act 1988

All rights reserved
No portion of this work may be copied
in any way without the prior written
permission of the publishers.

ISBN 978-1-912256-14-3

Printed by IngramSpark

Contents:

Contents	i
Acknowledgements	ii
Introduction	iii
Ackee	1
Bananas(Green)	3
Cho Cho	5
Dasheen	7
Egg plant	9
Fruit	11
Ginger	13
Hog Plum	15
Indian Kale	17
Jackfruit	19
Kidney Beans	21
Lime	23
Mango	25
Naseberry	27
Okra	29
Plantain	31
Quince	33
Radish	35
Sweet Potato	37
Tomato	39
Ugli	41
Vegetables	43
Water Melon	45
Yam	47
Zaboca	49
Glossary	51

Acknowledgements

Many thanks to the people who helped in the compilation and revision of this book, with special thanks to Jim Sullivan, Ermine Benjamin and Chris Day.

Dedicated to my grandaughter, Maitlyn and my son Pianki (Mark)

Introduction

This book contains a series of illustrations of fruits and vegetables from different parts of the world which are available to people in England.

When Mark(Pianki) visited the local markets in London he saw many fruits and vegetables such as mangoes, bananas, zaboca, plantains and pineapples. When he visited the markets in Bridgetown, Barbados and Kingston, Jamaica he was thrilled to find similar fruits and vegetables.

All the fruits and vegetables illustrated in this book are grown in the Caribbean even though most of them originated in places such as Africa, The Americas and India. Cassava is one of the native foods of the Caribbean.

The variety of fruit and vegetables was taken to the Caribbean by explorers, colonisers and Africans who were enslaved.

The Caribbean is a group of islands surrounded on the west by the Caribbean Sea and on the east by the Atlantic Ocean.

The islands although generally very hot, vary in the amount of rainfall, prevailing winds, soil compositions, rock formation, topography and mineral wealth. These climatical and geographical factors affect the fruits and vegetables grown in the islands; for instance Jamaica grows a wider variety of mangoes than Barbados.

The foods mentioned in this book can all be found growing in different parts of the Caribbean Islands. It is possible to grow Caribbean foods in other parts of the world for example, tomatoes are gown in England, mangoes in India, yams in Africa and so on.

These foods can be bought in most large supermarkets and certain small shops world-wide. In England they are sold by many ethnic shops as well as major supermarkets These are generally available in markets such as Ridley Road, Walthamstow and Brixton in London as well as markets in Wolverhampton and Birmingham in the West Midlands.

Karlene Rickard
1999

A Guide to African Caribbean Foods From A to Z

*A*ckee was introduced to Jamaica during the 19th Century from West Africa and is now the national fruit of Jamaica.

Ackee is a fruit which is used as a vegetable. It grows on a tree with smooth bark and waxy leaves in countries where the climate is generally very hot, with seasonal rainy periods. The fruit ripens during the wet season when it bears the amazing red ridge-shaped pod which bursts at the tip to reveal three black stones attached to bright yellow flesh.

Ackee is rich in protein, vitamins B and C. Once cooked it can be eaten by itself or with salted cod fish also known as salt fish. Traditionally, it is cooked with salt fish in Jamaica.

Recipe

CURRIED ACKEE

You will need:

1 tin ackees
1 tablespoon curry powder
1 oz (28.5gm) margarine
2 oz (57gm) plain flour
1 medium onion
Salt
1/2 pint (28ml) coconut milk
lime juice

What to do:

Heat the margarine, add the curry powder. Peel and slice the onion and add to the curry mixture. Cook for five minutes. Stir in the flour. Add salt to taste. Open tin of ackees and drain off the liquid. Add the ackees to the curry sauce, add lime juice and simmer over a low heat for approximately 20 minutes until the ackees are tender.
Serve with plain rice.

Serves 4 people

A Guide to African Caribbean Foods From A to Z

Green banana is a starchy fruit. As it ripens the starch is changed into sugar. There are many varieties of bananas. They grow on a tall herbaceous plant. The largest banana is Lacatan. Bananas grow in a cluster called 'a hand'. There are usually six to seven hands arranged on a long stalk, which is called a bunch.

Bananas grow in tropical and sub-tropical regions where there is plenty of rainfall, one such island is Grenada.

Green bananas are rich in iron and starch and can only be eaten when cooked. They go well with salt fish.

RECIPE

BOILED BANANAS

YOU WILL NEED :

2 large or 3 small green bananas
Enough water to cover the bananas
Pinch of salt

WHAT TO DO :

Soak bananas in cold water beforehand. Peel bananas and cut into halvesBring the water to the boil, add the salt. Put peeled bananas in the boiling water. Cover and cook for 25 minutes, or until tender.

Serve with meat, fish or other vegetables

Green bananas can be boiled, deep or shallow fried.

Serves 4 people

A GUIDE TO AFRICAN CARIBBEAN FOODS FROM A TO Z

Cho Cho, also known as Chow Chow, Chayote and Christophene, is a fruit but it is used as a vegetable. It grows on very thick, green, broad leafy vines in very fertile soil. It is usually supported on a trellis or arbour so that the Cho Cho can hang comfortably. It is common in tropical and sub-tropical countries, where there are regular showers of rain. The colour ranges from pale green to cream.

Cho Cho is especially rich in vitamin A. It can be eaten raw, but more commonly cooked and eaten with meat, fish or by itself. It is delicious in soups. Cho Cho is plentiful in Trinidad and Jamaica.

RECIPE

Cho Cho

YOU WILL NEED :

1 cho cho
Pinch of salt

WHAT TO DO :

Peel the cho cho. Cut into quarters. Bring the water to the boil and add a pinch of salt. Add segments of cho cho. Boil until tender. Serve with meat, fish.or cooked vegetables

Cho Cho is a member of the melon family and can either eaten boiled or baked.

Serves 2 people

A Guide to African Caribbean Foods From A to Z

Dasheen, also known as Coco, white Eddoe and Slip-and-dip, is a vegetable, which grows as a tuber underground in rich black swampy soil. It is found in tropical regions. Dasheens can be used to make a delicious soup.

Dasheen must be cooked before it can be eaten . It is a very popular food in Caribbean soups.Serve with meat or fish.

Dasheen contains small amounts of carbohydrate, fibre and vitamins. The leaves are very rich in vitamin A and calcium.

Recipe

Dasheen Pudding

You will need:

375gm dasheen
1 oz (28.5gm) margarine
1/4 pint (14ml) milk
Salt to taste
2 eggs separated

What to do:

Cook the dasheen in boiling water until tender. Mash the dasheen with butter, milk, pepper salt and slightly beaten egg yolks. Blend and beat the mixture until light. Whisk the egg whites very stiffly, fold into the mixture and pour into a buttered dish. Leave about 2.5 centimetres from the top. Bake in a moderate oven for about 30 minutes until the pudding has risen to the top.

Serves 4 people

A Guide to African Caribbean Foods From A to Z

Egg plant, also known as mélange and aubergine is a fruit. It grows on runner vines in warm temperate fertile regions where there is plenty of rain. Eggplant is common throughout the Caribbean. The fruit can be purple, white or yellow. It is used as a vegetable. In Trinidad they are used to make 'fritters' called baigani. Eggplant is mainly water with very little nutritional value. .

Recipe

Egg Plant Salad

You will need:

250 gm (1/2lb) egg plant
1 small onion finely chopped
1 small garlic crushed
1 cup tomatoes juice
½ tablespoon olive oil
½ tomato paste
¼ teaspoon sugar
½ tablespoon vinegar
Salt and pepper.to taste
½ cup celery finely chopped.

What to do:

Peel and cut eggplant into 2cm (1 inch) cubes. Heat oil in a heavy saucepan and then saute the eggplant until soft.
Drain well and place on a absorbent paper until the sauce is ready.
Saute onion and garlic in oil in a saucepan until soft.
Stir in tomato paste and tomato juice.
Add vinegar, sugar and salt. Simmer for 5 minutes. Drain and stir in eggplant and celery into the sauce.
Serve chilled.

Serves 2 people

A Guide to African Caribbean Foods From A to Z

The fruit of a plant is the fleshy material covering the seed or seeds. Some fruits are made up of several smaller units, each containing a seed for example the jackfruit. In others, the seeds join together to form a single fruit, for example tomatoes and figs.

There are many different types of fruit grown in the Caribbean. There are over twenty varieties of mangoes in Jamaica example Julie, Blackie, Common and East Indian.

Recipe

Pouched Fruit

You will need:

1 Guava
½ Pineapple
1 small Paw paw)
1 Mango (not over ripe)
2 cups water
2 tablespoons lemon juice

What to do:

Cut into cubes three cups of fruit. Put the water and lemon juice in a saucepan to boil. Simmer for about three minutes. Add the prepared fruit. Keep simmering till the fruit is just soft. Remove from heat, drain off the syrup. When cool, return to fruit to the syrup.

Serves 3-4 people

A Guide to African Caribbean Foods From A to Z

Ginger is a root crop which grows underground in large clumps. It is an annual plant which grows mostly in tropical and sub-tropical regions, for example, in Grenada. The root is planted before the rainy season. Ginger is used as a spice. It is often ground with black pepper for seasoning, but can be used in cakes, biscuits and tea.

Ginger beer is very popular in the Caribbean. Jamaican ginger beer is a favourite drink in the UK, amongst African Caribbean people. Ginger beer can be bought in cans and bottles.

RECIPE

Gingerade

YOU WILL NEED :

Juice of 6 limes
2 tablespoons of cold water
4 slices of green ginger peeled and washed
5 cloves
1 teaspoon of whole allspice
2 pints (110ml) of boiling water
1/4lb (69 gm) granulated sugar

WHAT TO DO :

Pour the lime Juice into a large bowl.
Add 2 tablespoons of cold water. Add ginger to juice and water.
Add the clove and allspice and granulated sugar.
Pour in 2 pints (110ml) of boiling water allow to sit until the sugar dissolves. Chill for 15 minutes.

Serves 4 people

| A GUIDE TO AFRICAN CARIBBEAN FOODS FROM A TO Z |

Hog plum is a fruit that grows on very large tall dedicuous trees. It is an annual fruit, which becomes available when the climate is hot and wet.

Hog plum is common in Jamaica. It has a sweet pungent smell when ripe. It contains a fair amount of vitamins A and C. Hog plum is also rich in calcium.

The skin of the fruit can also be eaten. It is can used to make jelly.

RECIPE

Hog Plums Jelly

YOU WILL NEED :

1 lb (454.9 gm) hog plums
water
4 oz (138.5 gm) sugar

WHAT TO DO :

Wash the plums well. Place them in a saucepan with enough water to cover. Bring to the boil. Lower the heat and simmer for about thirty minutes. Strain the fruit from the juice. Do not crush the plums.
Bring to the boil again, continue to boil rapidly until the mixture reaches the setting point. Transfer the juice to a warm sterilised jar.

A GUIDE TO AFRICAN CARIBBEAN FOODS FROM A TO Z

Indian Kale is a vegetable which belongs to the cabbage family. It grows in temperate regions where the climate is warm with regular periods of rain.

Kale is found in tropical countries and is popular in Guyana. When cooked it can be eaten with meat or fish. It is rich in protein and vitamins.

Recipe

Indian kale In Butter

You will need :

1/4 lb (137gm) Indian Kale
1/2 oz (14.25) butter
pinch of salt
black pepper
nutmeg (pinch)

What to do :

Wash the indian kale properly in lots of water. Chop into small pieces and boil in a large or medium sized pan until tender. Remove the pan from the heat and drain the Indian kale in a colander. Heat the margarine until it begins to sizzle. Add the well drained indian kale and mix it thoroughly with the margarine.
Add salt, pepper and nutmeg to taste.
Serve immediately.

Serves 2 people

A Guide to African Caribbean Foods From A to Z

Jackfruit is an incredibly large fruit which can weight up to 70lbs (28kg). It has many segments, each with its own seed. It develops at the start of the rainy season. The trees grow in tropical countries such as Barbados.

The fruit can be eaten raw or cooked. When ripe the sweet segments are pulled from the core and eaten or used in curried dishes. The seeds can also be eaten and are very nutritious.

Jackfruit contains small amounts of calcium vitamin C and carbohydrates.

RECIPE

Jackfuit Salad

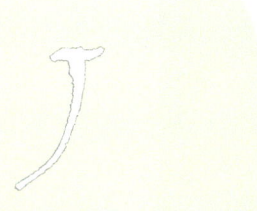

You will need :

1 tin or 1/8 Fresh Jackfuit
1 medium ripe banana
1 medium orange
some fresh cream

What to do :

Peel and slice the banana and put into a bowl. Peel orange, remove pith and cut into segments. Place flesh of orange on top of the banana slices. Open the tin of jackfruit, pour it on top of the banana slices and mix together. Chill for 15 minutes and serve with fresh cream. Can be served with mango ice cream.

Serves 4 people

| A Guide to African Caribbean Foods From A to Z |

Kidney Beans, also known as red beans, are pulses. They grow in pods on small shrubs. Kidney beans are planted in the dry season, just before the spring rains. They like fertile open, sunny soil.

They are grown throughout the Caribbean in such places as St Vincent. They are extremely rich in protein, iron and calcium. Kidney beans can be cooked with rice. When cooked with rice it is known as "rice n' peas" in Jamaica or "peas n' rice" in most of the caribbean. The beans are also delicious in pea soup.

RECIPE

RICE & PEAS

YOU WILL NEED :

4 oz (116.5ml) red peas
8 oz (226gm) rice
Few sprigs of thyme
1oz (28gm) coconut cream
1 clove garlic
1 small onion
salt & pepper to taste
2 pints (114mls) hot water

WHAT TO DO :

Heat the peas and put them in one quart (228ml) of water with the coconut cream and boil until tender. Add the salt, thyme and pepper. Add the clove of garlic slightly bruised. Wash the rice and add it. The water should cover the rice by about 2.5cm (1inch). Stir to prevent sticking. As soon as it starts to boil turn to a low heat, cover and leave to cook for 30 minutes.

Serve with meat and/or vegetables.

Serves 3-4 people

A Guide to African Caribbean Foods From A to Z

*L*ime is a fruit which is smaller and more acidic than lemon. It is grown on evergreen trees with small heart shaped leaves. The fruit is grown for its juice and for the oil in the skin. In the Caribbean lime is usually ready for use when the season is fairly wet. It is plentiful in Dominica. It is a popular fruit all over the world. In the Caribbean, it is used to make a long, refreshing drink called Lemonade or lime drink.

Lime contains small amounts of carbohydrate, protein and iron, and it is quite high in calcium and vitamin C.

RECIPE

Lime Drink

YOU WILL NEED :

1.5 litres water
4 limes
2ozs (56.25gm) sugar

WHAT TO DO :

Pour the water into a jug. Juice the limes into the jug. Add the sugar. Mix well until the sugar is dissolved. Can be served with ice.

Serves 4 people

A Guide to African Caribbean Foods From A to Z

Mango is a fruit which grows on deciduous trees. Most mango trees are extremely large, with leathery leaves and thick trunks.

In Jamaica there are many varieties of mangoess exampe East Indian and Julie. St. Lucia has more varieties of mangoes than most places. They have different shapes and sizes. The most common fruit shape is kidney-shaped. When the fruit is ripe, its skin can be light green, pinkish or different shades of yellow, lightly flicked with black depending on the variety.

Mango has a juicy fibrous yellow flesh. Some are more fibrous than others. Ripe mango is used in fruit salads, but pureed cooked or uncooked it is used in ice-cream and gelatin desserts. Unripe mangoes are used in chutney. Mango is rich in vitamins A and C.

RECIPE

Mango - Ice cream

YOU WILL NEED :

8ozs (225gm) castor sugar
4 tablespoons of water
4 ripe medium mangoes
strained juice of 1 lime
3/4 pint (42.75ml) of double
cream lightly whipped
pinch of cream of tartar

WHAT TO DO :

Mix the cream of tartar and sugar with the water. Bring to the boil and cook over a low heat, stirring until the syrup thickens. Peel, remove stones and sieve mangoes. (They should produce about 1/2 pint (28.5ml) of puree.) Add the mango puree to the syrup with the lime juice. Stir in the cream until well blended. Turn into freezing tray and freeze. When half- frozen, remove from refrigerator and stir until firm.

Serves 4 people

A Guide to African Caribbean Foods From A to Z

Naseberry, also known as Sapodilla, is a fruit. The tree is generally tall and slender. It comes from South America. The flesh when ripe is brown and sweet. It surrounds a large black seed. Ripe naseberry has a taste similar to dates.

Naseberry is popular in Jamaica. It is rich in carbohydrates and vitamins.

Recipe

Naseberry Jelly

You will need:

100 ml water
2 tablespoons gelatin
1-3 litre naseberry juice
4 ozs (125g) ginger

What to do:

Heat the water. Sprinkle in the gelatin stirring until it has completely dissolved.
Remove the mixture from the heat. Add the juice, stir well. Taste, then add sugar if necessary. Stir again until dissolved. Place the whole mixture to set in a refrigerator.

Serves 3-4 people

A GUIDE TO AFRICAN CARIBBEAN FOODS FROM A TO Z

Okra (ochra), also known as ladies fingers, is a fruit. Okra grows annually on shrubs. It was introduced to the Caribbean Islands in the eighteenth century. It is used in soup and stews. In Barbados, it is a vital part of their traditional dish Cou Cou.

Okra is rich in calcium and vitamin A and C.

Recipe

Stewed Okras

You will need :

1oz (28gm) margarine
10 okras cut in rings
1 large tomato chopped
1 onion sliced
salt and pepper

What to do :

Heat the margarine in a frying pan and sauté onion and okra rings. Add the tomato, season with salt and pepper and continue cooking over a low heat stirring regularly until the vegetables are tender and the mixture thickened.
Serve with meat and rice.

Serves 4 people

A Guide to African Caribbean Foods From A to Z

Plantain is a starchy fruit. It is much larger than a banana and has 3-4 ridges. Plantains grow on a succulent tree trunk, in bunches which are divided into hands. It is very common in tropical and sub-tropical regions, such as Martinique.

Plantains need a spell of heavy rain to grow successfully. The fruit can be fried, boiled, baked or grilled. It is a popular breakfast dish, with fish, in the Caribbean.

It is rich in vitamins A and C.

It is green when young and yellow when ripe.

RECIPE

YOU WILL NEED:

Plantain- Chips

2 ripe plantains
2ozs (56gm) plain flour
1oz (28gm) cinnamon
1oz (28gm) margarine

WHAT TO DO:

Peel plantains and slice length ways. Cut into chips. Mix flour with cinnamon. Heat the margarine. Dust chips with the cinnamon mixture and fry quickly in the margarine. Drain and serve hot or cold.

Serves 3 - 4 people

| A Guide to African Caribbean Foods From A to Z |

Quince is a fruit. It is grown on small deciduous trees (4-5 metres high) in regions where the climate is moderate. It likes deep fertile and well-drained soil. Although found in the Caribbean it is not common.

Quince used to be extremely popular in England in making marmalade.

It contains vitamins A and C.

Recipe

Quince Jam

You will need:

1lb (454gm) quinces
½lb (275gm) sugar
juice of 1 lemon
1 pint water

What to do:

First, prepare the quince by peeling, coring and chopping them into small pieces. Put the small pieces in a saucepan. Add enough water to cover the pieces. Cook slowly until the fruit is soft, about 20-30 minutes. Add the sugar and lemon juice. Bring to the boil and continue to cook until setting point is reached. Leave to cool and bottle. The boiling jam should be poured into a hot jar and covered with a clean cloth. When partly cool cover with grease proof paper. Store bottle in a cool place.

A Guide to African Caribbean Foods From A to Z

Radish is a small fleshy root vegetable. There are many types which vary in shape and colour. For example, there are black, white, pink and purple varieties.

Radishes are grown in regions where it is warm, with sufficient rainfall. They thrive in many parts of England, but are also grown in Jamaica. They are particularly rich in protein and are often eaten uncooked in salads.

RECIPE

Radish Salad

YOU WILL NEED :

2ozs (56gm) radishes
2ozs (56gm) spinach
1 tablespoon salad dressing
pinch of salt and pepper

WHAT TO DO :

Wash the radishes, remove the tops and roots. Thinly slice into rings. Wash the spinach thoroughly. Remove any thick centre stems. Place the spinach and three quarters of the radish rings in a glass serving dish. Toss in the salad dressing and season to taste with salt and pepper. Decorate the top of salad with the remaining radish rings. Serve with other salad dishes as an alternative to lettuce.

A Guide to African Caribbean Foods From A to Z

Sweet potato also known as potatoes is a starchy plant contrary to popular belief. It is not related to the King Edward's potato. It is grown underground but produces a trailing green plant above the surface.

To grow well, it needs a good deal of warmth and rainfall. It can be found in tropical regions such as Guyana. There is a large variety of sweet potatoes some with pink skin others with white, red or even purple.

Sweet potatoes are mostly long and globular and the flesh varies in colour from white to yellow and is often tender and sweet.

The pale variety has a small amount of most nutrients, but the deep orange variety is extremely rich in vitamin A.

RECIPE

You will need :

What to do :

Baked Sweet Potatoes

2 medium sized sweet potatoes
1oz (28.5gm) butter

Par boil the potatoes in boiling water for about 10 minutes. Drain, peel and slice. Arrange the slices of sweet potatoes in a greased dish. Spread butter over the potatoes. Bake in a moderate oven for half an hour. Serve with a meat dish. Sweet potatoes can also be roasted or boiled.

Serves 4 people

A Guide to African Caribbean Foods From A to Z

Tomato is a fruit, but is often used as a vegetable. It is grown on small soft shrubs in temperate regions. In St. Elizabeth, Jamaica, a large quantity of tomatoes are grown.

There are many varieties of the tomato; some have yellow flesh others red.

The fruit is often used in salads, but adds a delicious flavour to most dishes and can be stuffed with meat or fish.

Tomato is rich in vitamins A and C.

RECIPE

Stuffed Tomatoes

YOU WILL NEED :

2 large tomatoes
Pinch of salt and pepper
1oz (28gm) fresh wholemeal bread crumbs
1 small onion finely chopped
1 garlic clove crushed
1oz (28gm) mushrooms finely chopped
4 blanched almonds finely chopped
pinch of chopped parsley
1 tablespoon margarine

WHAT TO DO :

Cut the tomatoes into halves, scoop out the middle part and keep. Turn the tomato shells upside down and drain. Strain the seeds from the tomato flesh and blend the pulp with the rest of the ingredients. Put the mixture into the tomato cases. Put a small knob of margarine on top of each and place in an oven-proof dish. Bake in a pre-heated oven, (gas mark 4) for about 20 minutes or until golden brown.
Serve with grilled vegetable or fish.

Serves 2 people

A Guide to African Caribbean Foods From A to Z

*U*gli, also known as Tangelo and Bilva, is a cross between a grapefruit and a tangerine. It takes its unfortunate name because it has an unusual shape, but has a delicious taste.

Ugli grows on trees in tropical countries such as Jamaica.

The fruit is usually eaten fresh and can be used in salads or citrus drinks. The skin provides a scent which is highly valued for flavouring. Ugli is rich in vitamins.

RECIPE

Ugli Fruit Salad

YOU WILL NEED :

1 ugli
1 banana (small)
1 apple
Handful of grapes
1 apricot
orange juice or lime juice

WHAT TO DO :

Peel ugli and break into segments. Wash and slice apple, pear, grapes and apricot. Peel and slice the banana, add to other fruits. Sprinkle with lemon juice to prevent them from browning.
Mix all the fruits together. Arrange attractively in the bowl. Add a little orange or lime juice. Cover with foil and chill in the refrigerator for about one hour. Can be served with mango ice-cream.

Serves 4 people

| A Guide to African Caribbean Foods From A to Z |

Vegetable is a term used to describe the edible parts of some plants, mostly the roots and leaves, but also the stems. Carrots, eddoes are edible roots; spinach and kale are leaves and rhubarb is a stem. Vegetables contain a range of nutrients, protein, fat, starch, vitamins and minerals.

RECIPE

Vegetable Soup

You will need:

1lb (450gm) calalou,   2ozs (56gm) okra
6ozs (56gm) egg-plant (aubergine) peeled and coarsely chopped
1 tablespoon vegetable oil
2ozs (56gm) lean salt pork cut into 1/2 cubes
1 green banana peeled and chopped
1 clove garlic,   1/4 tablespoon thyme
pinch ground cloves
1/2 tablespoon chopped chives
1/2 tablespoon fresh hot peppers, seeded and chopped
tablespoon white vinegar, coconut milk
1/2 pint (28.5ml) water

What to do:

Wash, drain and coarsely chop the greens. Place in a large heavy saucepan with the okra, egg-plant and water. Cover and cook until vegetables are tender. Put to one side. In the heavy dish, heat the oil and fry the salted pork lightly. Cover and cook gently until the bananas and onions are tender. Add the rest of the ingredients and cook for a few minutes longer. Take out the cubes of salted pork and preserve. Rub the mixture through a sieve. Add the cooked vegetable mixture and beat thoroughly until you have a light puree. If the mixture is thick, add some water. Return the cube of pork to the casserole and heat through. The soup should be a thick smooth puree.

Serves 3-4 people

Water melon is a large fruit. It grows on a vine which runs along the surface of the ground with small roots securing the vine to the soil.

Water melon is juicy and refreshing. It needs a hot atmosphere with regular rainfall to grow successfully. The fruit is fairly fibrous.

There are many varieties. They are popular in Trinidad.

The fruit as its name suggests is mostly water, but contains essential vitamins and minerals.

RECIPE

Water Melon Dessert

YOU WILL NEED:

1/2 medium sized melon
3/4 litres water
4 small pieces of ginger
a pinch of cinnamon
1/2 tablespoon allspice
1 spoons sugar

WHAT TO DO:

Halve and quarter the melon. Remove the seeds. Peel the rind off very thinly. Put the flesh in a saucepan with the water, ginger and spices. Bring to boil until the melon is tender. Drain the juice and add the sugar. Stir until dissolved. Add the fruit, ginger and spices. Bring to boil and simmer for a further 15 minutes. Throw away pieces of ginger. Pack melon into a hot sterilised jar, filled with boiling syrup. Seal and store.

Serves 4 people

| A Guide to African Caribbean Foods From A to Z |

Yam is a starchy tuber it grows underground the Yam vine grows above the surface and is usually long with small, shiny heart-shaped leaves. There is a large variety of yams they vary in size. The flesh may be white, yellow or purple. They grown in tropical and sub-tropical regions. They are usually planted in the dry seasons, just before regular showers of rain. Yams can be found all over the Caribbean, and are very popular in St. Vincent.

Yams must be cooked before they can be eaten. They are commonly used in soups, but can also be baked or fried.

Yams contain small quantity of most nutrients but quite a lot of carbohydrate.

RECIPE

YAM CAKES

YOU WILL NEED:

3 tea cups of mashed cooked yam (1 1/2 lbs or 675gm)
2 tablespoons of grated onion
1 egg
salt and pepper to taste
1/2 cup of flour
Sun flower oil

WHAT TO DO:

Mash the cooked yam. Beat the egg. Put the mashed yam in a bowl and add the onion, beaten egg and salt and pepper, mix well. Shape the mixture into small cakes and roll in the flour. Fry in hot oil on both sides until golden brown.

Serve with fish and vegetables.
Serves 2-3 people

A Guide to African Caribbean Foods From A to Z

Zaboca, also known as avocado and pear, is a fruit which was introduced to the Caribbean from South America. Zaboca grows in tropical and sub-tropical countries on deciduous trees which vary in size. Zaboca is popular throughout the Caribbean, example Trinidad. There are many varieties with skins ranging from green to black.

Zaboca is nutritious; it is very rich in vitamins, and proteins. The flesh of a ripe zaboca is yellowy- green when ripe. At the centre is a large seed. It can be used in salads, eaten with rice and peas or crushed and used as a paste on bread or biscuits.

A Guide of African Caribbean Food From A to Z

ZABOCA DIP

You will need :

1 medium zaboca (avocado)
3 tablespoons mayonnaise
2 tablespoons lime juice
1 tablespoon grated onion
pinch of salt

What to do :

Cut the zaboca in halves length ways, remove the stone, but do not throw it away. Scoop out the green flesh, mash to a paste, add ingredients and blend well. Put the stone back in the mixture to prevent discolourisation. Chill well.

www.ingramcontent.com/pod-product-compliance
Lightning Source LLC
Chambersburg PA
CBHW042122100526
44587CB00025B/4151